Gardens

By Heather Hammonds

Illustrations by Ben Spiby

T0342757

Contents

The Messy Garden

It was Saturday morning.
Tara and Mum were up early,
because they were going to visit Aunty Meg.

"Aunty Meg lives by herself now," said Mum.
"She needs us to help her with her garden."

Aunty Meg was pleased to see them.
"My garden is a mess," she said.

There was long grass
growing everywhere.
And the flower gardens
were full of weeds.

"There's a lot of work to do,"
said Tara.

5

Mum cut the long grass and plants.
Aunty Meg raked up the leaves.

Tara pulled out the weeds
and put them in garden bags.
Then she cleaned the old bird bath.

It was very hot work.

At the end of the day,
the garden was tidy again.

There were bees buzzing in the flowers,
and birds splashing in the clean water
in the bird bath.

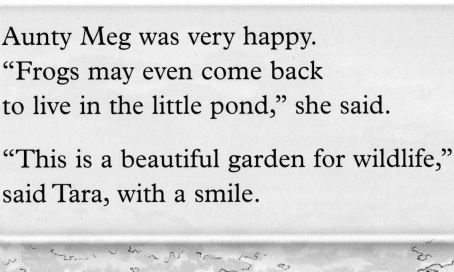

Aunty Meg was very happy.
"Frogs may even come back
to live in the little pond," she said.

"This is a beautiful garden for wildlife,"
said Tara, with a smile.

9

A Garden for Wildlife

I think it is good to have a garden for wildlife.

A garden should have lots of plants
and fresh water,
because birds, insects and frogs
will come and live there.

If a garden has trees and bushes,
birds can make their nests
in the branches.

Insects can hide in the bark.

Birds and insects can get food
from the flowers and berries.

A garden should have lots of plants, because bees get pollen and nectar from the flowers.

It is good to have a bird bath in a garden
so that birds can drink or splash in it.

Frogs may come and live
in a garden pond.

A beautiful garden with wildlife
can make you feel happy.